Andrew Jackson

Childhoods of the Presidents

John Adams
George W. Bush
Bill Clinton
Ulysses S. Grant
Andrew Jackson
Thomas Jefferson
John F. Kennedy
Abraham Lincoln
James Madison
James Monroe
Ronald Reagan
Franklin D. Roosevelt
Theodore Roosevelt
Harry S. Truman
George Washington
Woodrow Wilson

Andrew Jackson

Daniel E. Harmon

Mason Crest Publishers
Philadelphia

Produced by OTTN Publishing, Stockton, New Jersey

Mason Crest Publishers
370 Reed Road
Broomall, PA 19008
www.masoncrest.com

Copyright © 2003 by Mason Crest Publishers. All rights reserved. Printed and bound in the Hashemite Kingdom of Jordan.

First printing

1 3 5 7 9 8 6 4 2

Library of Congress Cataloging-in-Publication Data

Harmon, Daniel E.
   Andrew Jackson / Daniel E. Harmon.
     p. cm. (Childhood of the presidents)
   Summary: A biography of the seventh president of the United States, focusing on his childhood and young adulthood.
   Includes bibliographical references and index.
    ISBN 1-59084-274-X
   1. Jackson, Andrew, 1767-1845—Childhood and youth—Juvenile literature. 2. Jackson, Andrew, 1767-1845—Juvenile literature.
3. Presidents—United States—Biography—Juvenile literature.
[1. Jackson, Andrew, 1767-1845—Childhood and youth.
2. Presidents.] I. Title. II. Series.
E382.H27 2003
973.5'6'092—dc21
[B]   2002069240

Publisher's note: All quotations in this book come from original sources, and contain the spelling and grammatical inconsistencies of the original text.

Childhoods of the Presidents

Table of Contents

Introduction 6
Arthur M. Schlesinger, jr.

A Child of the Frontier 9

Mischievous Andy 13

The Colonists Go to War 19

Andy Is on His Own 29

Andy Jackson's Career 37

Chronology 42

Glossary 43

Further Reading 44

Internet Resources 45

Index 46

★ *Introduction* ★

Alexis de Tocqueville began his great work *Democracy in America* with a discourse on childhood. If we are to understand the prejudices, the habits and the passions that will rule a man's life, Tocqueville said, we must watch the baby in his mother's arms; we must see the first images that the world casts upon the mirror of his mind; we must hear the first words that awaken his sleeping powers of thought. "The entire man," he wrote, "is, so to speak, to be seen in the cradle of the child."

That is why these books on the childhoods of the American presidents are so much to the point. And, as our history shows, a great variety of childhoods can lead to the White House. The record confirms the ancient adage that every American boy, no matter how unpromising his beginnings, can aspire to the presidency. Soon, one hopes, the adage will be extended to include every American girl.

All our presidents thus far have been white males who, within the limits of their gender, reflect the diversity of American life. They were born in nineteen of our states; eight of the last thirteen presidents were born west of the Mississippi. Of all our presidents, Abraham Lincoln had the least promising childhood, yet he became our greatest presi-

Introduction

dent. Oddly enough, presidents who are children of privilege sometimes feel an obligation to reform society in order to give children of poverty a better break. And, with Lincoln the great exception, presidents who are children of poverty sometimes feel that there is no need to reform a society that has enabled them to rise from privation to the summit.

Does schooling make a difference? Harry S. Truman, the only twentieth-century president never to attend college, is generally accounted a near-great president. Actually nine—more than one fifth—of our presidents never went to college at all, including such luminaries as George Washington, Andrew Jackson and Grover Cleveland. But, Truman aside, all the non-college men held the highest office before the twentieth century, and, given the increasing complexity of life, a college education will unquestionably be a necessity in the twenty-first century.

Every reader of this book, girls included, has a right to aspire to the presidency. As you survey the childhoods of those who made it, try to figure out the qualities that brought them to the White House. I would suggest that among those qualities are ambition, determination, discipline, education—and luck.

—*ARTHUR M. SCHLESINGER, JR.*

A Child of the Frontier

In 1776, nine-year-old Andy Jackson stood in the village square, surrounded by his relatives and neighbors. Their attention was on him as he read the latest news from Philadelphia, Pennsylvania. Most of the people listening to Andy couldn't read. They were all settlers living in "the Waxhaws," a *frontier* area on the border of North and South Carolina. They depended on a few people, often school-age children, to read aloud newspapers brought on horseback from large cities. The news was often weeks or months old by the time it arrived.

On this day, however, Andy wasn't just reading the news. He was reading an important new document, the Declaration of Independence. It had recently been adopted and published by American colonial leaders in Philadelphia. The settlers knew the Declaration was going to have a lasting, serious impact on their lives. It meant war against England.

Titled *Carolina Home*, this early illustration gives some idea of the hardships endured by settlers along the Waxhaws frontier of North and South Carolina. Andrew Jackson's childhood there was made even more difficult by the untimely death of his father.

At that time, life was already difficult for young Andrew Jackson. His parents were Scotch-Irish *immigrants* from Carrickfergus, a seaport on the rocky coast of Northern Ireland. Most researchers think the Jacksons arrived in the American colonies in 1765. Here, they hoped to find a more promising future than poor people could expect in their homeland. Andy's father was named Andrew, his mother Elizabeth.

The details of Andy's birth are cloaked in mystery. No records are available to prove where in America the Jacksons' ship landed. They may have arrived at Charleston, South Carolina, the colonies' major southern seaport, or at one of the northern ports, perhaps in Pennsylvania. In addition, no birth certificate for Andrew Jackson exists. Historians have argued about Jackson's birthplace since he became a national hero during the War of 1812. It was most likely South Carolina—especially since Jackson himself said he was born there.

Most researchers agree that Andy's young parents were living in the Waxhaws settlement at the time of his birth. "Waxhaw" was the name of a Native American tribe that once roamed the area. The controversy over Andy's birth centers on the question of where in the Waxhaws, exactly, the cabin in which he was born was situated. (A few historians slyly suggest the cabin may have been right on the border between the two Carolinas, so the question of his birth state would depend on precisely where the bed was placed inside the home.)

What is known for certain is that soon after coming to America, the Jacksons traveled far inland to the Waxhaws, 160 miles from Charleston. Several of Elizabeth Jackson's sisters already had settled there with their husbands and families.

A Child of the Frontier

They were prospering by the time the Jacksons arrived. But Andrew and Elizabeth found that the best land in the area

> Andrew Jackson was the first American president born in a log cabin.

had already been taken, so they settled on an unattractive plot of 200 acres beside a creek near the Catawba River. It is believed the Jacksons did not own the land, but leased it in hopes of someday being able to buy it.

Andy never knew his father. Three weeks before Andy's birth on March 15, 1767, the elder Andrew Jackson died unexpectedly. Possibly he was killed in an accident, but some say he simply worked himself to death clearing the land and trying to start a farm in the clay-soiled, pine-thick wilderness. Historians believe he was not yet 30 when he died.

Elizabeth realized she could not keep up the fledgling farm with her small sons, Hugh and Robert, and the newborn infant Andrew. The Jacksons were forced to move into the nearby home of their cousins, the William Crawford family. Mrs. Crawford was in poor health, so Elizabeth took over much of the housework.

Thus, Andy Jackson began life in a household where he was almost an outsider. The Jacksons were made welcome by their relatives—indeed, Elizabeth became indispensable in managing the home. But it was a meager start. At a very young age, Andy learned that if he were to make something of his life, he would have no family fortune on which to build. He would have to rely on himself.

2

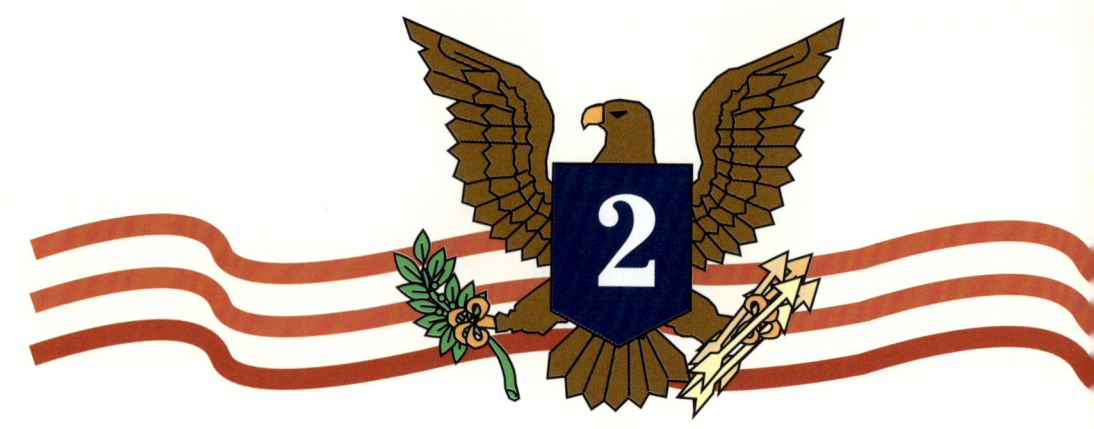

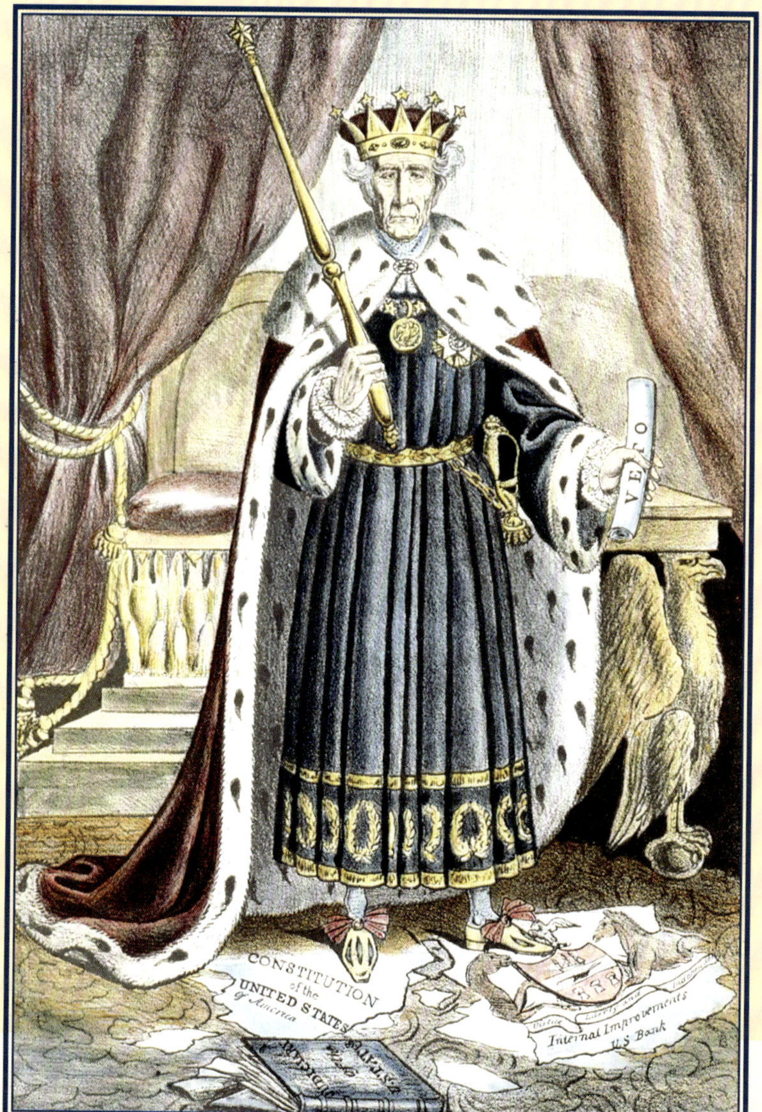
VETO
CONSTITUTION of the UNITED STATES of America
Internal Improvements
U.S Bank

Mischievous Andy

The Crawford home was crowded and lively, with eight Crawford children for the Jackson boys to play with. The whole settlement was a busy place. Farmers grew large crops of corn, barley, and *indigo* and raised cattle. With the profits they earned at market, they bought more land and built nicer homes.

Frontier life would hardly appeal to children today. For breakfast, farm families usually ate fresh-baked cornbread or a dish of boiled, mashed cornmeal called mush. For dinner and supper they had wild game the men and youths had shot on forest hunts, meat from cattle and hogs they raised and butchered themselves, and vegetables they grew in their gardens and fields. They built their cabins near a stream or spring so they could have fresh running water nearby. There, they washed their clothes and drew water in buckets for drinking,

Childhood acquaintances would remember the young Andy Jackson as bad-tempered, combative, and occasionally mean-spirited. Later in life, a political cartoonist would play on such unflattering aspects of President Jackson's personality, depicting him as a tyrannical king.

cooking, and bathing. Even in icy winter weather, youngsters had the task of drawing water from the creek throughout the day and bringing it inside. There were no indoor bathrooms, and the outhouse typically was some distance from the living quarters.

Candles and the single large fireplace provided the only light at night. Lighting was of little concern, though, for most settlers went to bed very early, by today's standards, since they had to rise before dawn the next morning and set about their work. The women sewed and dyed clothes for the family. The men cleared trees and plowed the fields. As for the children, there always were chores to do, from chopping and carrying firewood to helping cook, work the fields, and tend cattle.

Meanwhile, there was ample time for playing and exploring the wilderness. From early childhood, Andy was a particularly lively fellow. He also grew to be a relentless prankster. The red-haired, freckle-faced, blue-eyed youngster constantly got himself into trouble because of his tricks and his quick temper. He often fought—not just to defend himself or his honor, but from something of a mean streak that would mark much of his life even as an adult. Many youths of the neighborhood found it hard to get along with Andy. Some of his childhood acquaintances would later remember him as a bully—but not toward younger, weaker children. Oddly, he often picked on youths older than himself. He was not afraid to fight them. He would rush to the defense of smaller children who were being mistreated.

Perhaps Andy's tendency to take offense easily was brought about by an unfortunate childhood condition.

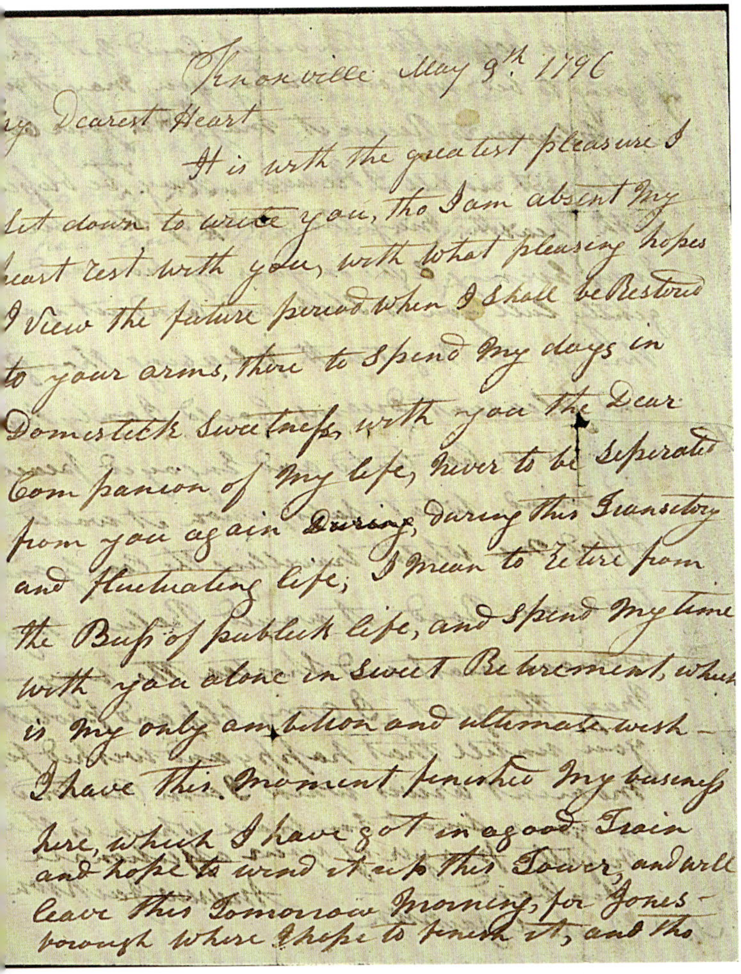

Knoxville May 9th 1796
My Dearest Heart
It is with the greatest pleasure I
sit down to write you, tho I am absent my
heart rest with you, with what pleasing hopes
I View the future period when I shall be Restored
to your arms, there to Spend my days in
Domestick Sweetness with you the Dear
Companion of my life, never to be Seperated
from you again During during this Transitory
and fluctuating life; I mean to Retire from
the Buss of publick life, and Spend my time
with you alone in Sweet Retirement, which
is my only ambition and ultimate wish –
I have this moment finished my business
here, which I have got in a good Train
and hope to wind it up this Tower, and will
leave this Tomorrow Morning, for Jones-
borough where I hope to finish it, and tho

Although he hated school, Andy Jackson learned to read and write, which was somewhat uncommon for settlers in the Waxhaws district. Seen here is the first page of a letter he wrote to his wife, dated May 9, 1796.

Historians report that as a boy, Andy could not help drooling at the mouth. The other children quickly learned not to laugh at Andy for "slobbering." If they did, he pounced on them like a tiger.

Another reason for his sensitive, insecure feelings may have been that his family had no land. Most Waxhaws settlers, while not rich, at least owned their farms. Mrs. Jackson did not. She and her sons in effect were being taken care of by relatives. This undoubtedly caused some of the other youngsters

16 Andrew Jackson

Andy, like other frontier boys, assumed a good deal of responsibility at an early age. When he was 11, he helped drive cattle from the Waxhaws to Charleston, a journey of many days.

to look down on Andy and his brothers—and prompted Andy to challenge them whenever he sensed this attitude.

Once, mischievous friends reportedly handed the unsuspecting Andy a musket to shoot. They had overloaded it with gunpowder. He didn't realize the "kick" would be so powerful against his shoulder when he pulled the trigger. Bystanders thought it amusing when he was knocked to the ground—but they dared not laugh, for he leaped to his feet and threatened to beat anyone who did.

Andy loved to wrestle with other youngsters, to challenge them in high jumping, and especially to race them, either on foot or horseback. A fierce competitor, he hated to lose a race or tussling match. He was not a very successful wrestler, but that never discouraged him. Even when larger, stronger boys threw him to the ground, he amazed them by getting right up and charging back into the contest. One childhood schoolmate later remembered, "He would never stay throwed."

Mrs. Jackson tried to interest her son in becoming a minister at an early age. She sent him to school at the Waxhaw Presbyterian Church when he was five years old. She knew he would have a better chance of a happy life if he learned to read and write—abilities most people living on the American frontier did not possess. But Andy saw school as an ordeal, not an opportunity. One biographer has suggested Andrew Jackson may have been the least educated of all American presidents, not necessarily because of the quality of the frontier school or any lack of intelligence on Andy's part, but because his heart wasn't in "book learning." What he wanted to be doing, rather than studying, was roaming the forest. He didn't like to write. He especially hated spelling lessons and was a horrible speller even as an adult.

> In 1806, Andrew Jackson killed lawyer Charles Dickinson in a pistol duel. Dickinson had called him a cowardly scoundrel and insulted his wife.

Surprisingly, though, Andy liked to read. He also demonstrated an early ability as a public speaker, one who could persuade people with his passionate feelings and ideas. He didn't express himself with big words or even with proper grammar. His everyday language, like that of many American frontier dwellers, was sometimes salted with *profanity*. But he was believable. Later, to the plain, poor workers of late 18th- and early 19th-century America, that would mean a lot more than flowery, empty speeches.

The Colonists Go to War

War was brewing in the mid-1770s as Andy struggled through his first years of formal education. Many *colonists* in America didn't like the policies of England, the ruling country—especially when it came to taxation. Increasingly, Americans believed they were being taxed unfairly and were not receiving worthwhile benefits in return. They had no voice in how much they were taxed or in how the British government spent their tax money.

In the lower colonies, homesteaders like the Crawfords and Jacksons were caught up in the growing spirit of independence. They weren't bothered much by King George's taxes on tea and stamps, which drove many other colonists to fury. But many of the frontier settlers agreed wholeheartedly with their city-dwelling counterparts that the time had come to break away from English control. This was especially true among

The young Andrew Jackson helped his mother tend to the horribly wounded victims of the Waxhaws Massacre, an infamous 1780 incident during which British soldiers under the command of Banastre Tarleton stabbed and slashed hundreds of American militiamen who were trying to surrender.

poor Irish families like the Jacksons, whose ancestors in Ireland had long suffered harsh treatment at the hands of British masters.

By the time Andy read the Declaration of Independence in 1776, fighting had already begun. The first skirmishes had been fought in Massachusetts the year before. One of Andy's cousins, Robert Crawford, was in a *militia* that had gone to Charleston to help protect that important seaport from a British invasion.

At first, there was little fighting around the Waxhaws, but tension and quarreling kept neighbors on edge. Some colonists remained loyal to the British king despite the Declaration of Independence, while their neighbors wanted the British to leave. Bands of *Tories*—settlers who supported the British king—spied on the activities of neighboring *Patriots* like the Crawfords and Jacksons. Patriots were those colonists who supported the Revolution.

Tories joined red-coated British troops in skirmishes and full-scale battles against rebel militiamen and trained *Continental Army* soldiers. More skirmishes and battles are believed to have been fought in South Carolina than in any other colony during the Revolution. Although they rarely had much impact on the final outcome of the war, they're especially notable because in some of them, no British soldiers participated at all. They were waged by Americans on both sides—often neighbor against neighbor and even cousin against cousin.

In 1779, 16-year-old Hugh Jackson, Andy's oldest brother, joined the Continental Army. He saw action only once, at the

The Colonists Go to War 21

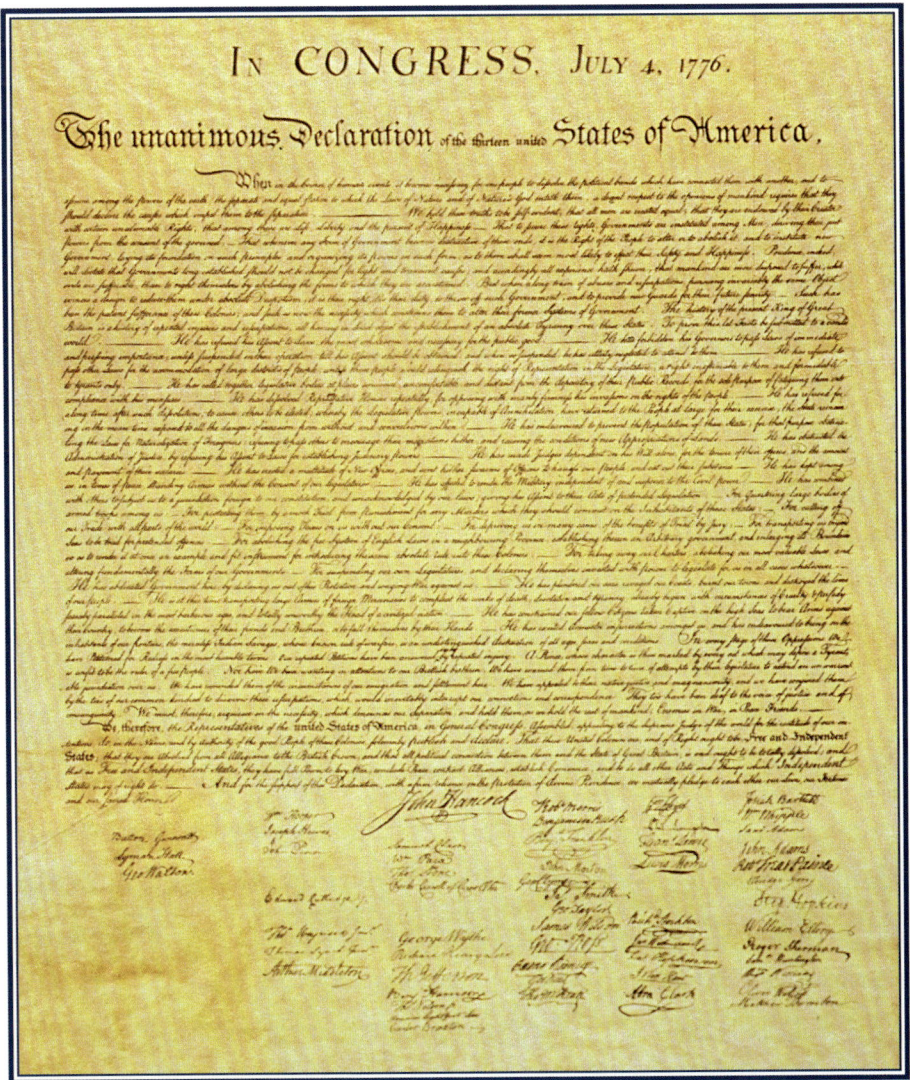

The Declaration of Independence. When nine-year-old Andrew Jackson read aloud a copy of the document for his relatives and neighbors, everyone realized that war with Great Britain was inevitable.

Battle of Stono Ferry near Charleston. Hugh died of **heatstroke** after the battle.

Soon afterward, a British cavalry (horseback) force commanded by Lieutenant Colonel Banastre Tarleton arrived in

22   Andrew Jackson

Residents of the Waxhaws may have paid little notice to the first shots of the American Revolution, which were fired in far-off Lexington, Massachusetts, on April 19, 1775. But bitter fighting would eventually come to their doorsteps.

northern South Carolina. They raided Patriot farms and scoured the countryside tracking down members of the colonial militia. Not far from the Waxhaws, they ambushed Colonel Abraham Buford's militia band. More than 100 Americans died—many of them struck down with swords after they had tried to surrender. Tarleton, whose nickname among his enemies was "Bloody Ban," had lived up to his terrible reputation.

Robert and Andy Jackson helped their mother tend to some of the wounded who retreated to the Waxhaws church. The boys cringed at the horrible injuries they saw and shuddered as they listened to groaning survivors recount the slaughter. Historian James Parton later wrote, "The men were dreadfully mangled. Some had received as many as thirteen wounds, and none less than three."

Families of the Waxhaws, like others throughout the colonies, lived in constant fear. For long periods, all the able-bodied men of the farm households—and many of the older boys—were away fighting. Mothers and children left at home kept constant vigil, dreading the sudden approach of raiders. This became the way of life for many colonists, both Tories and Patriots.

Robert, then 16, and Andy, 13, joined the Patriot cause in 1780. They were part of a cavalry unit commanded by Colonel William R. Davie. Historians doubt that Andy actually participated in serious battles. Because of his age, the militia commanders assigned him to be a messenger and camp helper. He knew the Waxhaws and surrounding lands thoroughly, and he made himself quite useful in Davie's service.

In time, Andy saw his share of danger. In fact, he once came within an inch of death by the sword. It happened in April 1781, shortly after a battle. Tories had surprised and scattered the Patriots. After spending a night hiding in the wilderness, weary and famished, Robert and Andy rode to the cabin of one of their relatives. They tied their horses in the woods and went inside. The animals were not well concealed. A Tory neighbor found them and reported to the local British commander. Thinking the horses might belong to militia fighters, English forces broke into the Crawford cabin. They were annoyed to discover that the "militiamen" they expected to find inside were mere boys, and they angrily set about ransacking the home.

24   Andrew Jackson

While British troops plundered the house, abused the family, and searched for American soldiers who might be hiding nearby, an angry officer glared at Andy. He demanded that the youngster clean his boots, spattered with mud from the swamps through which he'd ridden. The *feisty* lad refused. He demanded to be treated as a prisoner of war, which meant he could not be forced to perform servants' duties. This infuriated the soldier. Without a second thought, the officer drew his sword from its scabbard and swung it viciously. Andy was able to deflect it only partially with his hand. The sharp blade slashed his fingers and face. Then the officer directed a savage slash at Robert.

For the rest of his life, Andrew Jackson bitterly wore the scars of the British officer and bore in his heart a hatred for the British army.

Next, the British took the Jackson brothers, one of their cousins, and about 20 other Americans as prisoners to a *stockade* at Camden, South Carolina, about 40 miles south of the Waxhaws. Wartime prison camps are awful places even today. In centuries past, they were generally worse. During the Revolution, both the British and American armies acquired appalling reputations for either mistreating their prisoners or ignoring them, letting them weaken and die in misery.

The Jacksons and their comrades were fed poorly—just a few crusts of stale bread. There were no beds and not enough blankets to keep away the chill at night. Their injuries went untreated. Both Andy and Robert were suffering from serious wounds that became infected. Their captors separated them, so each could not know whether the other was alive or dead.

The Colonists Go to War

They lived in filth. To make matters worse, they caught *small-pox*, a deadly disease that ravaged the Camden stockade.

Then came hope. A large American force arrived in the area and took a position on nearby Hobkirk's Hill. From the stockade, Andy could see the friendly army's camp. They had come to take Camden from the British, but strangely, they didn't attack. Why not? Andy wondered impatiently. They obviously outnumbered the defending *redcoats*.

Unhappily for the American commander, he had to wait for his *artillery* (cannons) to arrive before he could lay siege to

Andy Jackson, "the brave boy of the Waxhaws," raises his hand to block a sword slash in this 19th-century lithograph. Andy, whose hand and face were seriously cut by the blow, had angered the officer by refusing to clean his boots.

the British stronghold. To charge across open fields against protected, well-trained British soldiers would have been foolhardy. Once the big guns came up, he could pound the English into submission. A day and night passed. Andy and his cellmates wished the Americans would attack soon and set them free.

The British commander did not wait for the foe to increase in strength. He ordered a surprise attack on Hobkirk's Hill early one morning. The Americans were sent reeling in disarray. The prisoners' hopes for rescue were dashed.

Andy and Robert were dying of fever when their mother came to their rescue not long after the *fiasco* of Hobkirk's Hill. She persuaded their captors to include the boys in a prisoner exchange that was being arranged. Some of the captured Patriots, including Robert and Andy, were released in return for some British soldiers who had been captured by the Americans.

The journey back home to the Waxhaws was as torturous to the brothers as prison. Some of their clothes and their shoes had been stolen, and a miserable, chilly rain drenched them. Their mother had managed to provide only two horses. She rode one, and Robert—so weak he couldn't walk—rode the other. Andy hobbled behind them in his bare feet. The young men were exhausted and deathly ill by the time they arrived at the

> **Andy later wrote of his bout with smallpox:**
> "When it left me, I was a skeleton—not quite six feet long and a little over six inches thick! It took me all the rest of that year to recover my strength and get flesh enough to hide my bones."

Waxhaws. Robert soon died. Andy was delirious with fever. He barely recovered from the ordeal, nursed for weeks by his mother.

Besides the loss of his older brothers in the fight for independence, Andy would soon lose his mother. Near the end of the war, Elizabeth went to Charleston to help nurse American captives aboard British prison ships in the harbor. She understood the risk. Ships at anchor, especially those that housed prisoners in filthy conditions, often bred epidemics, contagious illnesses that spread rapidly among crowded populations. Elizabeth Jackson fell fatally sick of *cholera*, a dreaded disease also known as "ship fever" because it spread so easily and caused such devastation in the cramped confines of a ship's hold.

Andy later described how devastated he felt when he learned of her death, saying, "I felt utterly alone, and tried to recall her last words to me." He especially agonized over the news that she had been buried in an unmarked grave outside Charleston. He would never be able to find her burial site.

Elizabeth Jackson had sacrificed two sons, a husband, and her own life for America. Throughout the rest of his life, Andy firmly believed his mother was a truly great Patriot.

A view of Charleston, South Carolina, in the 1780s, around the time Andy Jackson went to the port city to claim a sizable sum of money he had inherited upon the death of a relative in Ireland. Unfortunately, the youth left Charleston penniless, having lost his inheritance gambling.

Andy Is on His Own

Andy Jackson was just 15 years old as the American Revolution drew to an end, but for all practical purposes, he was a man. His parents and brothers were dead; he was alone. "His youth was burnt up in the war," wrote historian Gerald W. Johnson, "and he jumped straight from infancy to manhood."

The tall, bony youngster lived with various relatives in the Waxhaws and set to work to earn money. Andy was not afraid of work. Growing up in a farming community, he had early learned to tend cattle and crops. At age 11, he had helped drive a herd of cattle from the Waxhaws to sell in Charleston—a journey of many days.

Perhaps a greater difficulty for the maturing boy was managing his temper. In at least one situation, he left his relatives' care after quarreling with another member of the household. Andy was staying at the home of Robert Crawford, who had served as an American major in the Revolution. Also lodging with the Crawfords was a young captain named Galbraith, who talked in a thick Scottish accent. When Andy one day teased him because of his accent, Galbraith threatened to horsewhip the lad. Andy had never flinched from an older or bigger challenger, and he had no intention of doing so now. He defiantly told the officer that if he intended to use the whip, he'd best be prepared for the afterlife. The fight was avoided, probably because Major Crawford stepped between them, but the tension it caused was too great for Andy to remain in the Crawfords' care for long.

Andy went to work as an apprentice, or student helper, to another relative who was a saddle maker. Then, on the strength of his reading ability, he taught school for more than a year while still in his teens.

But Andy's yearning for freedom, fun, and adventure was overwhelming. He had become fond of sport and betting. The earliest known example of Andy's writing, dated March 22, 1779, was a note to himself on "how to feed a Cock" (a trained, fighting rooster upon which money would be wagered). Andy's prefight diet for a fighting bird: "some Pickle Beaf Cut fine."

Young Andy during these years received an unexpected bit of good fortune. A relative in Ireland died, leaving him approximately $1,500. In the 1780s, this was a great sum—many years' wages, for most common folk. Would Andy buy land with the money? His relatives and neighbors hoped he would invest in a large tract and become a prosperous young farmer.

But no—Andy foolishly believed he could turn his *inheritance* into a lifetime fortune by "investing" it in gambling. When he went to Charleston and claimed his inheritance, he began gambling at cards and cock fighting. Andy was also

Andy Is on His Own

very fond of horse races. After spending some of his money on flashy new clothes, he bet the rest of it on horses . . . and lost.

Incredibly, Andy had squandered his sizable fortune in a matter of days. He didn't even have enough money left to pay the keeper of the inn where he had taken a room. Desperately, he entered a tavern and placed one final bet in a dice game. The wager: his horse, the only thing he had left, against $200. If he lost, he would be not only homeless and penniless in a boisterous port city, but a debtor as well—and he was only in his mid-teens!

This time, the dice settled in his favor. He took his comparatively meager winnings, paid the innkeeper, and rode home in shame to the Waxhaws. He had thrown away his inheritance, and he knew he would be scorned by those who'd expected him to return as a well-to-do youth. The only thing he had gained from his journey was an important lesson, learned the hard way. Many years later, he remarked that it was the last time in his life he ever played dice.

Riding home forlornly through the forests, Andy thought about his future. He realized he could never establish himself as a worthy citizen of the newly independent nation if he continued to behave so recklessly. But how could he make a good living, now that his money was all gone and he was entering manhood? He enjoyed books. He resolved to take up the study of one kind of book in particular: a book of law.

It was December 1784. In those times, America had no law schools. To become a lawyer, a young man found an established lawyer willing to teach him. The youngster would "read law" under the tutor's guidance. When he knew enough to pass the state *bar* (legal) examination, he was qualified to "hang out his shingle" as a lawyer. The law was much less complicated then than it is today, and bar exams weren't so difficult to pass. But it did require quite a bit of reading.

For his mentor, Andy found a lawyer named Spruce Macay, who practiced in Salisbury, North Carolina, about 75 miles from the Waxhaws. Andy rented a bedroom at the town's Rowan House, a tavern. While living there and reading law, Andy continued his wild ways. He was the life of the tavern by night, drinking bourbon whiskey and gambling.

Now a lanky six feet tall, he became an excellent horseman and sharpshooter. Some of the good citizens of Salisbury later expressed bewilderment that such a wild young man would one day be elected president. One remembered him as a "mischievous fellow, . . . the head of all the rowdies hereabouts." He was by no means the churchgoing type—although in later years, as a national leader, he expressed a deep reverence for God.

As always, he was ready for sporting competition at every opportunity. On one occasion, a local man of remarkable strength, Hugh Montgomery, is said to have challenged Andy to a quarter-mile footrace. Montgomery realized that although he was far more powerful than his opponent, the agile Andy was easily the faster runner. Montgomery suggested a way to make the race fair. Andy would give him a head start—half the distance to the finish line. To balance this great advantage, Montgomery would carry a rider piggyback.

Many townspeople turned out to witness such an outrageous contest. To their delight, swift Andy Jackson caught up

Andy Is on His Own

One resident of Salisbury, North Carolina, where the young Andy Jackson studied law, recalled the future president as "the head of all the rowdies hereabouts." Yet throughout his life ordinary people were drawn to Jackson—and he to them. Here townsfolk turn out to wish him well on his way to the White House.

with Montgomery and his human burden just short of the finish and won by several steps. Everyone thought it was a great show—except the poor piggyback rider. Montgomery, intent on winning, had gripped his legs so tightly that the man was in serious pain.

Another event Salisbury citizens would remember long after Andy left was the night he and his friends tore the tavern apart in a joyful but costly celebration. It's an old custom to break the liquor glasses after drinking a toast on very special occasions. The noble idea is that the glasses must never in the

Andrew Jackson

In the early 1800s, dueling was an accepted way for gentlemen to settle disputes involving their reputation or honor. Never one to suffer insults calmly, Andrew Jackson killed a lawyer in a duel after the man had spoken ill of him and his wife, Rachel.

future be used for a less worthy toast.

On this particular evening, Andy and his pals ended their party by drinking a toast and dashing the glasses to bits. By that time, unhappily, they had already had far too many drinks. They apparently decided their table should also be destroyed so it could never again be used for a less meaningful celebration. Then they went on a gleeful rampage, breaking all the furniture and ripping the window curtains. The shocked citizens of Salisbury would not soon forget Andy Jackson and his brand of "fun."

When asked about his Salisbury years much later, while he was in the White House, Andy recalled simply, "Ah, I was but a raw lad then, but I did my best."

Despite his waywardness, Andy was serious about his legal studies. He worked at it for two years, reading the law book, running errands, and copying documents by hand for Macay. Then he studied for the better part of a year under Colonel John Stokes, one of the area's best-known lawyers. Stokes was a colorful showman in the courtroom. He had lost

Andy Is on His Own

a hand to a British swordsman during the Revolution and had replaced it with a silver doorknob. Courtroom audiences loved to watch Stokes hammer his knob-fist on the table.

Andy passed the bar exam and began to represent a variety of *clients*. He proved to be a natural at frontier law—although he didn't always win. In one of his early cases, before he was yet 20 years old, Andy reportedly represented a man charged with theft, guaranteeing victory in court. If he didn't get the man acquitted, he promised, the client wouldn't have to pay his lawyer's fee. The thief was convicted and Andy lost his earnings. Apparently, his luck at gambling had not changed since his Charleston disaster.

Andy loved acting out his clients' stories in court, and observers liked to see him in action. They were both entertained and impressed by his skills as a public speaker. He had a magnetic personality at social events as well. Nancy Jarret, a young woman who knew him in Salisbury, remembered that "his ways and manners were most captivating. . . . [T]here was something about him I cannot describe except to say that it was a *presence*."

But there were more than enough lawyers to handle disputes and financial matters in Salisbury, so Andy decided to follow the westward-moving frontier. With another young lawyer-judge named John McNairy, Andy set off to the west across the Smoky Mountains. Soon, he was a noted courtroom representative among the frontier folk around Nashville, Tennessee.

General Andrew Jackson, hero of the battles of Horseshoe Bend and New Orleans, in his dress uniform.

Andy Jackson's Career

Andrew Jackson's political career began in 1796 in the brand-new state of Tennessee. He was elected to serve as Tennessee's first congressional representative in Philadelphia, at that time the new nation's capital city. Just one year later, he was elected to the U.S. Senate. After only a few months in office, though, he resigned and became a judge with the Superior Court of Tennessee. Meanwhile, he was elected major general of the Tennessee Militia.

It was his service as commander of the Tennessee Militia during the War of 1812 against Great Britain that gave Andy national fame. In 1812 Andy was sent by the government to lead the fight against the pro-British Creek Indians in Georgia and Alabama. Andy gathered a force of friendly Native Americans to help his frontier soldiers against the Creeks. The climax came at the Battle of Horseshoe Bend on the Tallapoosa River in Alabama in 1814. There, Andy's forces routed the Creeks. As a result, vast wilderness lands—more than 20 million acres—were taken over by the United States.

American political leaders were impressed by what Andy had accomplished. They sent him to New Orleans, Louisiana,

A portrait of Andrew Jackson's wife, the former Rachel Donelson Robards. In the nasty 1828 presidential campaign, opponents tried to use the circumstances of Rachel's divorce nearly 40 years earlier to discredit Jackson.

to command the defense of that important port against British invasion. On January 8, 1815, he succeeded in repulsing a larger British force with almost no losses among his own men. The victory made Andrew Jackson a national hero and set the stage for his return to politics—this time in quest of the nation's highest office.

After fighting the Seminole Indians in southern Alabama and Georgia, Andy briefly served as governor of the Florida Territory. He soon returned home to Tennessee, but not for long. He spent the next two years representing his adopted state in the Senate before running for president in 1824.

As a presidential contender, Andy found his primary support among the common people, the working class. To refined society leaders and wealthy businessmen he was a "loose cannon," a somewhat unpredictable, independent statesman who couldn't be controlled. He was not well educated and, in the minds of many, he was not "respectable."

The election of 1824 was one of the most confusing in the nation's history. Jackson was one of four candidates. Given the nickname "Old Hickory" because of his reputation for hard-fighting toughness, he received more votes than anyone else—but not a majority. The outcome was then decided in the House of Representatives, and John Quincy Adams was named president.

Four years later, Andy was again a candidate. The campaign of 1828 was bitter. Adams's supporters attacked Jackson for his controversial marriage. In 1791—nearly 40 years earlier—Andy had married Rachel Donelson Robards, who had divorced her cruel first husband. Three years afterward, they had discovered that the divorce had not been legalized.

Andrew Jackson's decisive defeat of the British at the Battle of New Orleans, one of the few American victories in the War of 1812, made him a national hero. Ironically, the battle occurred several weeks after the United States and Great Britain had signed a peace treaty ending the war.

Andrew Jackson

> Andrew Jackson was the first president nominated as a candidate by a national political convention (1832).

They'd had to remarry—and to endure, for the rest of their lives, hurtful criticism that their courtship and marriage had been an unlawful scandal.

Despite these attacks, Andy won the election easily and became America's seventh president. Soon after the election, Rachel died of a heart attack. Andy believed her death was caused in part by the vicious nature of the campaign.

After burying Rachel at their Tennessee home, the Hermitage, he went to Washington to begin his first presidential term. In 1832, he was reelected.

While president, Andy Jackson often championed individual freedom and strong state governments, as opposed to an expanding federal government. Despite that, he governed with a firm hand. He didn't hesitate to fire members of his administration who disagreed with his policies, and he frequently used his veto power to block congressional bills. Presidential vetoes—the president's right to reject a new law passed by Congress—are common today, but in the early 1800s they were rare. During his time in office, Andy exercised the veto 12 times—more than the previous six presidents combined. For years afterward, other statesmen would follow the example Jackson set as a strong president who tested the balance of authority between the White House and Congress.

After completing his final White House term early in 1837, Andy—now almost 70—at last retired to the Hermitage, near Nashville. He died

> Andrew Jackson was the first president to ride in a train.

The Hermitage, the home of Andrew and Rachel Jackson, is located in Nashville, Tennessee. America's seventh president is buried in the garden, beside his wife.

there on June 8, 1845, and was buried beside Rachel in the Hermitage garden.

Although Andrew Jackson's frontier upbringing was simple and his education limited, he was a complex character—and an important one in American history. His story is one of hardships, follies, adventures, and great accomplishments. In the words of historian Gerald W. Johnson, "It was a roaring career, resounding to the roars of cheering multitudes, of musketry, of artillery. . . . He hated and loved and swore with a magnificence beyond all American experience."

Chronology

1767 Andrew Jackson is born on March 15, probably in the Waxhaws settlement of South Carolina.

1780 Along with his brother Robert, joins a cavalry unit fighting for American independence during the Revolutionary War.

1781 Wounded and captured by British; brother Robert and mother soon die of disease.

1787 After "reading law" for more than two years, becomes a lawyer.

1788 Moves to Nashville, Tennessee.

1791 Weds Rachel Donelson Robards; three years later, they must have the marriage performed again after learning the initial union was not legal.

1796 Elected Tennessee's first U.S. congressman.

1797 Elected to the U.S. Senate.

1798 Becomes a judge of the Superior Court of Tennessee.

1812–15 Becomes a national hero during the War of 1812 by winning the Battle of Horseshoe Bend in 1814 and the Battle of New Orleans in 1815.

1817–18 Leads U.S. troops during the Seminole Indian War.

1821 Appointed the first governor of the new Florida Territory.

1823 Elected U.S. senator from Tennessee.

1824 Loses his first campaign for president, despite winning the popular vote.

1828 Elected to his first term as president of the United States; wife, Rachel, dies.

1832 Reelected to presidency.

1837 Retires to his home in Tennessee.

1845 Dies in Tennessee on June 8.

Glossary

artillery—heavy guns, including cannons and mortars.

bar—all the lawyers qualified to practice in court.

cholera—a contagious, sometimes fatal intestinal disease.

client—an individual or organization that hires a lawyer.

colonist—a settler or citizen of a colony, or foreign territory.

Continental Army—the main army of the American colonies during the Revolution.

feisty—energetic and stubborn.

fiasco—a total failure.

frontier—the region at the fringe of settled territory.

heatstroke—a dangerous condition of high body temperature that can result from too much physical activity in hot weather.

immigrant—a person who leaves her or his homeland to live in a different country.

indigo—a plant grown for its use in a deep blue dye.

inheritance—money or property willed to a surviving person (usually a descendant) after the original possessor's death.

militia—a military unit composed of citizens who agree to serve for a short term in emergency situations.

Patriot—an American soldier or a supporter of the American cause during the Revolutionary War.

profanity—foul or disrespectful language.

redcoat—a British soldier during the Revolutionary War.

smallpox—a serious disease in which the body is covered with bumpy sores, or pox.

stockade—a military jail.

Tory—an American colonist who supported Great Britain during the Revolutionary War.

FURTHER READING

Booraem, Hendrik. *Young Hickory: The Making of Andrew Jackson*. Dallas: Taylor Trade Publishing, 2001.

Davis, Burke. *Old Hickory: A Life of Andrew Jackson*. New York: The Dial Press, 1977.

Kelly, C. Brian. *Best Little Stories from the American Revolution*. Nashville: Cumberland House, 1999.

Osinski, Alice. *Andrew Jackson, Seventh President of the United States*. Chicago: Children's Press, 1987.

Potts, Steve. *Andrew Jackson, A Photo-Illustrated Biography*. Mankato, Minn.: Bridgestone Books, 1996.

Quackenbush, Robert. *Who Let Muddy Boots into the White House?: A Story of Andrew Jackson*. New York: Prentice-Hall Books for Young Readers, 1986.

Stefoff, Rebecca. *Andrew Jackson, 7th President of the United States*. Ada, Okla.: Garrett Educational Corporation, 1988.

Internet Resources

- http://www.thehermitage.com
    The Hermitage (Andrew Jackson's Home in Tennessee)

- http://www.whitehouse.gov/history/presidents/aj7.html
    The White House History Section

- http://www.perigee.net/~mwaxhaw
    Museum of the Waxhaws and Andrew Jackson Memorial

- http://gi.grolier.com/presidents/aae/bios/07pjack.html
    Grolier Interactive

- http://www.infoplease.com/ipa/A0760592.html
    Infoplease.com (The Learning Network)

- http://www.potus.com/ajackson.html
    POTUS: Presidents of the United States

INDEX

Adams, John Quincy, 39
Alabama, 37, 38
American Revolution, 9, 19–27, 29, 35

Buford, Abraham, 22

Camden, South Carolina, 24, 25
Carrickfergus, Ireland, 10
Catawba River, 11
Charleston, South Carolina, 10, 20, 21, 27, 29, 30, 35
Continental Army, 20
Crawford, Robert, 20, 29, 30
Crawford, William, 11, 13, 19, 20, 23
Creek Indians, 37

Davie, William R., 23
Declaration of Independence, 9, 20

England, 9, 19

Florida Territory, 38

George III, king of England, 19
Georgia, 37, 38

Hermitage, the, 40–41
Hobkirk's Hill, 25, 26
Horseshoe Bend, battle of, 37

Ireland, 10, 20, 30

Jackson, Andrew "Old Hickory"
 and American Revolution, 9, 19–27, 29
 birth of, 10–11
 childhood of, 13, 14–15, 16–17, 29, 30
 death of, 40–41
 and loss of inheritance, 30–31
 political career of, 37–40, 41
 studies and practices law, 31–32, 34–35
 and War of 1812, 10, 37–38
Jackson, Andrew (father), 10, 11
Jackson, Elizabeth (mother), 10, 11, 15, 17, 26, 27
Jackson, Hugh (brother), 11, 20–21
Jackson, Rachel Donelson Robards (wife), 39–40, 41
Jackson, Robert (brother), 11, 23, 24, 26, 27
Jarret, Nancy, 35
Johnson, Gerald W., 29, 41

Macay, Spruce, 32, 34
Massachusetts, 20
Montgomery, Hugh, 32–33

Nashville, Tennessee, 35, 40
New Orleans, Louisiana, 37
North Carolina, 9, 32

Parton, James, 22
Patriots, 20, 22, 23, 26, 27
Philadelphia, 9, 37

Rowan House, 32

Salisbury, North Carolina, 32, 33, 34, 35
Seminole Indians, 38
Smoky Mountains, 35
South Carolina, 10, 20, 22, 24
Stokes, John, 34–35
Stono Ferry, battle of, 21
Superior Court of Tennessee, 37

Tarleton, Banastre "Bloody Ban," 21–22
Tennessee, 35, 37, 38, 40
Tennessee Militia, 37

46

Index

Tories, 20, 23

U.S. Senate, 37, 38

War of 1812, 10, 37–38

Waxhaw Presbyterian Church, 17, 22
Waxhaws, 9, 10, 15, 17, 20, 22, 23, 24, 26, 29, 31, 32
White House, 34, 40

Picture Credits

3:	Hulton/Archive	28:	Bettmann/Corbis
8:	North Wind Picture Archives	33:	North Wind Picture Archives
12:	Bettmann/Corbis	34:	North Wind Picture Archives
15:	The Hermitage: Home of President Andrew Jackson, Nashville, TN	36:	The Hermitage: Home of President Andrew Jackson, Nashville, TN
16:	North Wind Picture Archives	38:	The Hermitage: Home of President Andrew Jackson, Nashville, TN
18:	The Hermitage: Home of President Andrew Jackson, Nashville, TN	39:	North Wind Picture Archives
21:	Joseph Sohm; Visions of America/Corbis	41:	Kevin Fleming/Corbis
22:	Bettmann/Corbis		
25:	The Hermitage: Home of President Andrew Jackson, Nashville, TN		

Cover photos: (left and center) The Hermitage: Home of President Andrew Jackson, Nashville, TN; (right) North Wind Picture Archives

Contributors

ARTHUR M. SCHLESINGER JR. holds the Albert Schweitzer Chair in the Humanities at the Graduate Center of the City University of New York. He is the author of more than a dozen books, including *The Age of Jackson*; *The Vital Center*; *The Age of Roosevelt* (3 vols.); *A Thousand Days: John F. Kennedy in the White House*; *Robert Kennedy and His Times*; *The Cycles of American History*; and *The Imperial Presidency*. Professor Schlesinger served as Special Assistant to President Kennedy (1961–63). His numerous awards include the Pulitzer Prize for History; the Pulitzer Prize for Biography; two National Book Awards; the Bancroft Prize; and the American Academy of Arts and Letters Gold Medal for History.

DANIEL E. HARMON is an author and editor in Spartanburg, South Carolina. He has written more than 30 nonfiction books, one short story collection, and numerous magazine and newspaper articles. Harmon has served for many years as associate editor of *Sandlapper: The Magazine of South Carolina* and editor of *The Lawyer's PC*, a national computer newsletter published by West Group. His special interests include nautical history and folk music.